Bridgestone
BOOKS

World of Reptiles

Alligators

by Adele Richardson

Consultants:
The Staff of Reptile Gardens
Rapid City, South Dakota

Capstone
press

Mankato, Minnesota

Bridgestone Books are published by Capstone Press,
151 Good Counsel Drive, P.O. Box 669, Mankato, Minnesota 56002.
www.capstonepress.com

Library of Congress Cataloging-in-Publication Data
Richardson, Adele, 1966–
    Alligators / by Adele Richardson.
    p. cm.—(Bridgestone Books. World of reptiles)
    Includes bibliographical references and index.
    ISBN 0-7368-4326-4 (hardcover)
    1. Alligators—Juvenile literature. I. Title. II. Series.
QL666.C925R52 2006
597.98'4—dc22   2004027942

Summary: A brief introduction to alligators, discussing their characteristics, range, habitat, food,
    offspring, and dangers. Includes a range map, life cycle diagram, and amazing facts.

Editorial Credits
Shari Joffe, editor; Enoch Peterson, set designer; Biner Design, book designer; Patricia Rasch, illustrator;
    Jo Miller, photo researcher; Scott Thoms, photo editor

Photo Credits
Allen Blake Sheldon, 1
Bruce Coleman Inc./Jack Couffer, 12; John Shaw, cover
Corbis/David Muench, 10
Eda Rogers, 6
Nature Picture Library/Peter Scoones, 20
Tom & Pat Leeson, 4, 16
Visuals Unlimited/Arthur Morris, 18

Table of Contents

Alligators

The alligator is one of the fiercest **predators** of the swamp. It has strong jaws and 80 sharp teeth. When old teeth are lost or broken, new ones grow in their places. Alligators grow thousands of teeth during their lives.

Alligators are reptiles. Reptiles are **cold-blooded**. They have scales and grow from eggs.

Alligators are closely related to crocodiles. They look alike, but there is a way to tell them apart. Alligators have wide, rounded noses. Crocodiles' noses are longer and V-shaped.

◀ The American alligator is the largest reptile in North America.

What Alligators Look Like

Alligators have long bodies and short legs. Their thick skin is covered with horny scales called **scutes**. Alligators are usually black, brown, or gray.

An alligator's eyes, ears, and nose are on the top of its head. Alligators sneak up on **prey** by swimming with just their eyes, ears, and nose showing above the water.

Two kinds of alligators live in the world. American alligators grow to be 6 to 14 feet (1.8 to 4.3 meters) long. Chinese alligators are usually about 5 feet (1.5 meters) long.

◄ An alligator's tail is half the length of its entire body.

Alligator Range Map

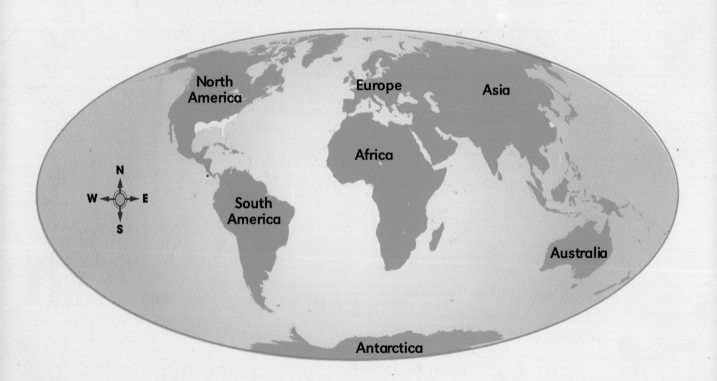

North America

Europe

Asia

Africa

South America

Australia

Antarctica

N
W E
S

☐ Where Alligators Live

Alligators in the World

American alligators live in the southeastern United States. Most are found in Florida and Louisiana. Alligators live as far north as North Carolina and as far west as Texas.

Chinese alligators live near the Yangtze River in eastern China. Most live in a place where alligators are protected. Only a few hundred Chinese alligators are left in the wild.

Alligator Habitats

Alligators live in **wetland** habitats. These wetlands include swamps, marshes, rivers, and lakes.

Many alligators make **burrows**. They use their tails, feet, and noses to dig deep holes in wet soil. They live in the burrows when the weather is too cold or too dry. Chinese alligators live where it is cool much of the year. They may spend six or seven months of the year in their burrows.

◀ Alligators live mainly in freshwater wetlands.

What Alligators Eat

An alligator will eat almost anything that crosses its path. Alligators eat fish, birds, and many other animals. Alligators do not chew their food. They tear off pieces and then swallow. Small animals are swallowed whole.

Most alligators hunt at night. They wait quietly for prey to come near. When an animal is close, the alligator leaps out of the water. It grabs the animal with its strong jaws. An alligator can leap 5 feet (1.5 meters) out of water to grab a bird perched on a tree branch.

◀ Fish are a big part of an alligator's diet.

The Life Cycle of an Alligator

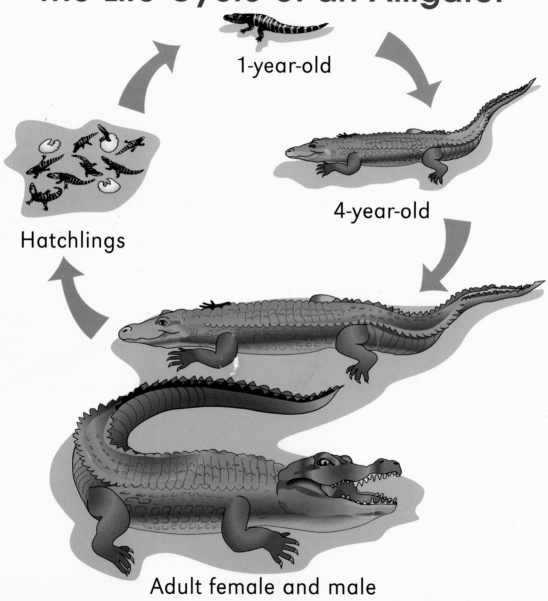

1-year-old

4-year-old

Hatchlings

Adult female and male

Producing Young

Alligators come together to **mate** in the spring or summer. After mating, the female builds a nest on dry land near water. She uses plants, leaves, and mud.

The female alligator lays 20 to 50 eggs. She stays nearby to guard the nest. The eggs hatch in about 65 days. The mother alligator breaks open the nest to help free the hatchlings. Then she picks them up in her mouth and takes them to water.

Growing Up

Alligators are about 8 inches (20 centimeters) long when they hatch. The young stay near their mother for up to two years. They often ride on their mother's head or back.

Young alligators grow up to 1 foot (30.5 centimeters) a year for the first six years of their lives. They hunt insects and small fish.

◀ A young alligator rides on its mother's head.

Dangers to Alligators

Young alligators have many predators. Larger alligators, raccoons, snakes, and large birds eat alligator young.

People are the biggest danger to American alligators. They build new roads and houses where alligators live. The alligators sometimes wander near people's homes and must be killed.

The Chinese alligator is **endangered**. Some Chinese alligators have been placed in zoos to keep them from dying out.

◄ People have pushed American alligators out of their habitats.

Amazing Facts about Alligators

- Alligators can hold their breath underwater for more than an hour.
- American alligators have been known to eat rocks, branches, and even tin cans.
- An alligator has a flap in its throat that closes when the alligator grabs food. The flap keeps the alligator from swallowing water.
- On land, alligators can run as fast as a horse for about 30 feet (9 meters).

◄ While underwater, an alligator can close its nose and ears to keep out water.

Glossary

burrow (BUR-oh)—a tunnel or a hole in the ground where an animal lives

cold-blooded (KOHLD-BLUHD-id)—an animal whose body temperature changes with the temperatures around it

endangered (en-DAYN-jurd)—at risk of dying out

mate (MAYT)—to join together to produce young

predator (PRED-uh-tur)—an animal that hunts other animals for food

prey (PRAY)—an animal hunted by another animal for food

scutes (SKOOTS)—horny scales that cover the skin of alligators and crocodiles

wetland (WET-luhnd)—area of land where the soil is covered with water

Read More

Kendell, Patricia. *Alligators.* In the Wild. Austin, Texas: Raintree Steck-Vaughn, 2003.

Swanson, Diane. *Alligators and Crocodiles.* Welcome to the World of Animals. Milwaukee: Gareth Stevens Publishers, 2004.

Internet Sites

FactHound offers a safe, fun way to find Internet sites related to this book. All of the sites on FactHound have been researched by our staff.

Here's how:
1. Visit *www.facthound.com*
2. Type in this special code **0736843264** for age-appropriate sites. Or enter a search word related to this book for a more general search.
3. Click on the **Fetch It** button.

FactHound will fetch the best sites for you!

Index